HUMBLE YOURSELF

Loren VanGalder

Spiritual Father Publications

Contents

Introduction

The 2013 Academy Award winner for best documentary is called *Searching for Sugar Man,* about a singer from Detroit named Rodriguez. With a style reminiscent of Bob Dylan, he made two critically acclaimed albums in the early seventies that went nowhere—and then he disappeared. A folk legend grew that he had committed suicide at a concert, either by shooting himself or setting himself on fire.

Meanwhile, someone brought his album to South Africa. Incredibly, he became a sensation in the anti-apartheid movement of the seventies. His albums sold millions, despite nobody knowing anything about him. Even more incredible, he was unaware of his popularity and never saw a penny from all those sales. After that brief recording career, he worked in the demolition and renovation of houses in some of Detroit's worst neighborhoods.

Finally, in the late 1990s, a record buff in South Africa decided to uncover the truth. He found Rodriguez in Detroit and brought him to South Africa, where he was welcomed as a hero and performed at sold-out concerts. Amazingly, fame did not seem to affect him. He gave away the money and returned to his work in Detroit, where he lived a modest life until he died in 2023. If you have a chance to see the movie, I think you will find it very inspiring.

God had a purpose in my watching that movie. It was more than an inspiring story. As I watched this humble man's reception in South Africa, I saw multitudes like him in the kingdom of God, unknown individuals going about a life of service, seeking neither fame nor notoriety. The Lord showed me that heaven is like South Africa was for Rodriguez. There is a cloud of witnesses and angels who are aware of these unsung heroes. One day, when they get to heaven, they will be applauded and their Lord will reward them for their labors.

The world constantly encourages self-exaltation. Even in church, the message is often about making it and being somebody. You don't hear much about humbling yourself, but Jesus said it is the key to being exalted. It takes courage, but are you willing to trust God and sincerely try to humble yourself?

Chapter 1

Humility Defined

"Everyone who exalts himself will be humbled, and he who humbles himself will be exalted." (Jesus, quoted in Luke 18:14)

You have probably heard that radical statement before, but have you ever taken it seriously? Or thought about what it really meant? How good are you at humbling yourself? Are you tired of exalting yourself, only to be humbled? Would you like God to exalt you?

At any given point, you have two options. You can exalt yourself, or you can humble yourself. If you don't humble yourself, God will do it for you. Sooner or later, if you insist on exalting yourself, you will be humbled. But if you humble yourself, the Lord promises to exalt you. It is a spiritual law established by God. Jesus is making a universal statement: this is for *everyone*. You are not exempt. There is no way around it.

Which way do you lean? Do you think you are humble? Do you *want* to be humble? It doesn't seem to be really popular, even among Christians. When was the last time you heard a sermon about humbling yourself? Doesn't it seem that even preachers focus on exalting yourself?

• "You're the head and not the tail!"

• "You are a son of the King!"

• "Go on in and take possession of your inheritance!"

If that is true in church, what about the world? Humility has a very negative connotation. In school and in the media, we are encouraged to assert ourselves. Humble people look like wimps. At home, parents encourage us to be somebody, to be successful. Few families seem to value humility.

So what is humility?

What does it mean to humble yourself, or exalt yourself?

Wikipedia says humility is the quality of being modest and respectful. It also gives a "Christian" definition: "A quality by which a person, considering his own defects, has a *humble opinion of himself* and *willingly submits himself* to God and to others for God's sake."

St. Thomas Aquinas said humility "consists in keeping oneself within one's own bounds, not reaching out to things above one, but submitting to one's superior." Kind of a mouthful, but interesting.

Merriam-Webster defines humble as not proud or haughty; not arrogant or assertive; not having or showing any feelings of superiority, self-assertiveness, or showiness. Instead, it reflects and expresses a spirit of deference or submission. It is the attitude of a person who acknowledges their failures and weaknesses, acting without pride and not boasting of their achievements.

How about synonyms for humble?

- Demure
- Lowly
- Meek
- Modest
- Unassuming
- Unpretentious

Other related words are:

- Compliant
- Unassertive
- Cowering
- Passive
- Timid
- Self-effacing

That's the adjective, now the verb. To humble is:
- To reduce to a lower standing in one's own eyes or in others' eyes.

- To make someone humble in spirit or manner.
- To destroy someone's power, independence, or prestige.

Look at the synonyms!

- Abase
- Demean
- Dishonor
- Humiliate
- Lower
- Shame
- Take down

Wow! No wonder people aren't jumping to take advantage of what Jesus offers! What man wants that? It is hardly surprising that the world wants nothing to do with this self-humbling! Fortunately, Jesus is not confined to some dictionary definition. His meaning is far richer and more profound.

Defining exalt

Before we look more closely at his understanding of humility, let's define exalt:

To raise someone to a higher rank or more powerful position; to elevate by praise or in estimation; to raise high. That is what God does for us if we humble ourselves!

Synonyms are *enthrone, glorify, honor, or magnify*. That is what we are supposed to do for God!

Jesus' teaching in Luke 18

With those definitions in mind, let's look at what Jesus was saying. He was talking to people who were confident in their own righteousness and looked down on everyone else. They were arrogant, self-righteous, and proud.

[10] "Two men went up to the temple to pray, one a Pharisee and the other a tax collector. [11] The Pharisee stood up and prayed about himself: 'God, I thank you that I am not like other people—robbers, evildoers, adulterers—or even like this tax collector. [12] I fast twice a week and give a tenth of all I get.'

"But the tax collector stood at a distance. He would not even look up to heaven, but beat his breast and said, 'God, have mercy on me, a sinner.'

"I tell you that this man, rather than the other, went home justified before God. For all those who exalt themselves will be humbled, and those who humble themselves will be exalted."

First, a Pharisee prays. Jesus says he prays *about himself*. The Amplified Bible says he *took his stand ostentatiously and began to pray thus before and with himself*. It really wasn't even a prayer. His main point seems to be reminding God—and those listening—of how great he was. He was exalting himself. In prayer, of all things. Pharisees were regarded as the most spiritual men of their day, yet he was blind to his sin and need for God. The person who exalts himself is unable to see who he really is before the Lord. He is deceived. Do we still have Pharisees today? Do you think some people still try to impress others with their prayers or spirituality?

Next came a tax collector, among the most hated men in that society, beating his chest and asking for mercy. He didn't even dare look up to heaven. He prayed sincerely, with no thought of impressing others. He humbled himself, and returned home right with God.

Jesus goes deeper

[15] People were also bringing babies to Jesus for him to place his hands on them. When the disciples saw this, they rebuked them. [16] But Jesus called the children to him and said, "Let the little children come to me, and do not hinder them, for the kingdom of God belongs to such as these. [17] Truly I tell you, anyone who will not receive the kingdom of God like a little child will never enter it."

I love the way God arranges things. It just so happened that as they sat there, thinking about what Jesus had said, some people brought their babies to him. The disciples, who failed to understand the lesson of the proud Pharisee, felt Jesus was above blessing babies. There were more important things to do, so they rebuked the parents. But Jesus says it is precisely the humility of a child that is *required* to enter the kingdom of God. His kingdom is not for the powerful or the rich, but for those who are like children. To enter the kingdom, we have to humble ourselves and become like a child.

Who are you more like? The Pharisee, feeling you have it all together and are better than others? The man aware of his sin and need for a Savior? Or a child who needs Jesus' touch and just longs to be with him? How can you humble yourself in your home today? At work? How are you tempted to exalt yourself?

Chapter 2

Taking the Lowest Place

(Luke 14)

¹One Sabbath, when Jesus went to eat in the house of a prominent Pharisee, he was being carefully watched. ² There in front of him was a man suffering from abnormal swelling of his body. ³ Jesus asked the Pharisees and experts in the law, "Is it lawful to heal on the Sabbath or not?" ⁴ But they remained silent. So taking hold of the man, he healed him and sent him on his way.

⁵ Then he asked them, "If one of you has a child or an ox that falls into a well on the Sabbath day, will you not immediately pull it out?" ⁶ And they had nothing to say.

This Pharisee didn't invite Jesus to dinner because he liked him so much, but to give him and his friends an opportunity to catch Jesus breaking the Sabbath. And wouldn't you know it, right in front of Jesus, there just happens to be a man suffering from dropsy. I love the way Jesus handled these situations. We could learn so much from him! He simply asks a well-chosen question to put the responsibility back on them. *"Is it lawful to heal on* the *Sabbath or not?"* Either they didn't know the answer, or knew it was a no-win situation. As often happened when Jesus confronted someone, they remained quiet. But their silence didn't keep Jesus from doing what was right. He answered his own question by healing the man. And they still had nothing to say, though you can be sure they were boiling inside.

[7] When he noticed how the guests picked the places of honor at the table, he told them this parable: [8] "When someone invites you to a wedding feast, do not take the place of honor, for a person more distinguished than you may have been invited. [9] If so, the host who invited both of you will come and say to you, 'Give this person your seat.' Then, humiliated, you will have to take the least important place. [10] But when you are invited, take the lowest place, so that when your host comes, he will say to you, 'Friend, move up to a better place.' Then you will be honored in the presence of all the other guests. [11] For all those who exalt themselves will be humbled, and those who humble themselves will be exalted."

Taking the highest place

Jesus doesn't leave things well enough alone. They were watching Jesus, and Jesus was watching them. He never seemed concerned about offending anyone or being politically correct. He had seen how the guests picked the places of honor at the table. Obviously, Jesus was not rushing to those places, nor was he offered one. In fact, they may have left the *least* important place for him. That wasn't what bothered him, though. It was what their actions revealed about their hearts.

You can learn a lot about people by simply observing them, as Jesus always did. I'm sure you have stood in line for food at a banquet. You may have noticed how some people subtly jockey for the best tables and rush to get in line first. They don't want to miss out on the best food. They are already eyeing the dessert table as they are getting their first plate. Other people let everyone else get in line first. This scene is repeated countless times in daily life. It is human nature to try to be first, to exalt oneself.

Is it sinful to sit in a place of honor? Certainly not! Jesus is seated at a place of highest honor, at the right hand of the Father! But he didn't clamor for that seat. His Father exalted him to that place because Jesus humbled himself. It is all about what is in our hearts and *how* you get to that seat. God knows if someone is maneuvering to appear humble, or is sincerely taking the lowest place to truly humble himself. The important thing is to be content with the lowest seat and not strive for the place of honor. The problem with seeking the best place is that someone else more deserving may come along and make you move, and you will be humiliated in front of everyone. If you take the lowest place, the only way you can move is up, and you will be honored in front of everyone.

Once again, the message is *"Everyone who exalts himself will be humbled, and he who humbles himself will be exalted"* (v. 11).

How to reap eternal rewards

Jesus seems to be the only one talking at this party! Nobody can contest his wisdom. Now he turns his attention to the host.

[12] Then Jesus said to his host, "When you give a luncheon or dinner, do not invite your friends, your brothers or sisters, your relatives, or your rich neighbors; if you do, they may invite you back and so you will be repaid. [13] But when you give a banquet, invite the poor, the crippled, the lame, the blind, [14] and you will be blessed. Although they cannot repay you, you will be repaid at the resurrection of the righteous."

As most of us would, this man had almost certainly invited his friends, family, and rich neighbors. Many prominent people of the town were there. He probably wanted to impress Jesus. But Jesus was not impressed. He says the dinner would have been far better if the poor, crippled, lame, and blind were invited. Why? Friends and family will probably return the favor and invite you over, and that will be your reward. But if you give to people who can't give in return, you will reap eternal rewards. Which would you rather have?

Jesus links humility with generosity. The proud person thinks about what he can get out of the situation. The humble person will be generous, thinking about others and their needs instead of himself. He will be especially drawn to people the world feels are unimportant. Are you generous? Look for opportunities to bless those less fortunate. Watch yourself this week to see when you go for the highest place. Try taking the lowest place and see how it feels.

Chapter 3

An Example of Exalting Yourself

J esus' harshest condemnation of the Pharisees is found in Matthew 23. Not surprisingly, once again we find him saying, *"whoever exalts himself will be humbled, and whoever humbles himself will be exalted."* It is a recurring theme in Jesus' teaching. The Pharisees were a great example of what it means to exalt yourself. Is it just a coincidence that they were also regarded as the most consistently spiritual men of their day? We would do well to study their lives and learn from their mistakes.

In verses 5–7, Jesus points out several examples of how they exalt themselves:

⁵ *"Everything they do is done for people to see: They make their phylacteries wide and the tassels on their garments long;* ⁶ *they love the place of honor at banquets and the most important seats in the synagogues;* ⁷ *they love to be greeted with respect in the marketplaces and to be called 'Rabbi' by others.*

- It was all about appearances. Would it make them look good? They weren't genuine.

- They tried to outdo each other with displays of religiosity. We don't use phylacteries and tassels today, but it could be the size of your Bible, how you dress, or your religious vocabulary.

- They loved the recognition that came from important seats at banquets and religious services.

- They loved being recognized in public and being called Rabbi, or in our case, "Pastor," or another religious title.

Jesus says they will be humbled. Do you want to avoid that? Humble yourself, so God can exalt you. Verses 8–10 give us clues on how:

8 "But you are not to be called 'Rabbi,' for you have one Teacher, and you are all brothers. 9 And do not call anyone on earth 'father,' for you have one Father, and he is in heaven. 10 Nor are you to be called instructors, for you have one Instructor, the Messiah.

Avoid the use of titles that make you look more important or spiritual than others. Be careful of the special privileges that pastors and Christian leaders may be offered or expect, such as a parking spot with your name on it next to the church entrance, or a sign in your car that gives you parking privileges at a hospital.

As followers of Christ, we are equals; we are brothers. We believe in a priesthood of all believers. Although there are different gifts and offices in the church, Jesus never intended for one to be exalted over the others. Be cautious about drawing attention to yourself, such as with your name in large letters on the church sign or prominently featuring your name and picture in newspaper or internet announcements. Who is more important in the church? Jesus, or the pastor?

It's great to aspire to greatness in the kingdom. Jesus says that the way to that greatness is to be the servant of all. In every situation, look for the opportunity to serve, not to be served.

People in the world tend to seek recognition, wealth, influence, position, and "things." Relationships are often evaluated according to how they benefit you.

Unfortunately, believers may not be that different. Jesus calls us to a lifestyle of humbling ourselves. Hopefully it becomes such a habit that it starts to feel natural, and suddenly we are much more aware of how people around us are exalting themselves. At work, in a restaurant, in line at a bank or supermarket, or in your car, always humble yourself. Take the lower place. Give preference to others.

God promises that as you do, he will exalt you.

Chapter 4

Suffering and Humility

Who better than the Apostle Peter to teach us about humility? Remember all the times Jesus had to humble him? Poor Peter. He reminds me of myself. Now he is older and wiser, and shares some of what he has learned.

Nobody enjoys suffering, yet Peter tells these suffering believers to *rejoice that you participate in the sufferings of Christ* (1 Peter 4:13). It is humbling to suffer. It is hard to exalt yourself when you are suffering. That is one of the main reasons God allows suffering in your life. And you may suffer *because* you humble yourself. Jesus suffered on the cross because he humbled himself and refused to defend himself against his accusers. Suffering also purifies us. Peter says, *It is time for judgment to begin with the family of God* (4:17). Peter is writing from experience. He was a witness of Christ's suffering, and has endured plenty of purifying and humbling himself. But if we humble ourselves with Christ and participate in his sufferings, we will have even greater joy as we share in his glory. *But rejoice inasmuch as you participate in the sufferings of*

Christ, so that you may be overjoyed when his glory is revealed (4:13).

Peter's appeal to the elders

To the elders among you, I appeal as a fellow elder and a witness of Christ's sufferings who also will share in the glory to be revealed: Be shepherds of God's flock that is under your care, watching over them— not because you must, but because you are willing, as God wants you to be; not pursuing dishonest gain, but eager to serve; not lording it over those entrusted to you, but being examples to the flock. And when the Chief Shepherd appears, you will receive the crown of glory that will never fade away (1 Pet. 5:1–4).

Elders in the church are to set an example for the younger men. Young people can easily spot someone drawing attention to himself and lifting himself up. Age may make that temptation more subtle, but it also makes it easier to deceive ourselves, thinking we are somehow beyond the sin of pride. Older men can become very skilled at making self-exaltation look spiritual. How can an elder stay humble?

- Maintain a shepherd's heart. The flock you are caring for is not yours, but God's. He has entrusted it to you, and you are responsible to him.

- Maintain a servant's heart. The excitement, challenge, and joy of serving can fade, along with the energy of youth. Despite that weariness, by serving willingly, we maintain a humble spirit.

- Be careful of greed. Financial security becomes a greater concern as we age. We need to maintain a humble dependence on the Lord and not exploit the people God has entrusted to us for our own financial gain.

- Make sure your daily life provides a good example. Don't let your knowledge and experience become an excuse to lord it over others.

Advice to young men

In the same way, you who are younger, submit yourselves to your elders. All of you, clothe yourselves with humility toward one another, because,

"God opposes the proud but shows favor (gives grace) to the humble."

Humble yourselves, therefore, under God's mighty hand, that he may lift you up in due time. Cast all your anxiety on him because he cares for you (1 Pet. 5:5–7).

A young man is full of passion and energy. He wants to prove himself and let the world know he is somebody. He's in competition with other men: for a woman, for a job, for success—even for a position in the church. But the Lord's command to the young man is: Be submissive to those who are older and clothe yourself with humility toward one another. Peter still remembers his struggles as a young man. He knows how hard it can be to submit to an older man. What young man is eager to clothe himself with humility? Or submit to others? He wants to clothe himself in strength, good looks, and an impressive presence! Young men tend to be rebels! But the young man who can humble himself and trust in God will see the Lord do tremendous things in his life. He can avoid having to be broken by the Lord after years of pridefully lifting himself up. Unfortunately, most of us are strong-willed and have to learn the hard way.

Humility is expressed in submission and the way we relate to others. Romans 13 teaches that humility is expressed through submission to every authority God has established, including the laws of the land, the police, your boss, and the pastor of your church. In this same letter (2:13–3:7), Peter speaks at length about submission. Are you serious about humbling yourself? Everywhere you go, look for who is in authority and make it a point to submit to that authority.

Is God against you?

Peter has a good reason for giving this instruction to the young men. He cites Proverbs 3:34: *God opposes the proud but gives grace to the humble.*

That is a fundamental principle of how God works. Do you see how close it is to what Jesus said?

God is opposed to (humbles) everyone who exalts himself (is proud), but gives grace (exalts) the humble (he who humbles himself).

If God is opposed to you, he is your enemy. You are fighting God. That is not an easy place to be. Sooner or later, God always wins, but you will suffer greatly in the process. It is much easier to have God as your friend. James says that friendship with the world is hatred toward God. Why? Because the world's system is all about pride and self-promotion. In the process, you become God's enemy. Do you feel like God is against you? Is it possible that because of your pride, you are fighting God? Humble yourself and surrender to God! In that way, you will receive the grace he promises.

God's grace is a gift. You cannot earn it. You don't deserve it. It is unmerited favor. An important part of humbling yourself is reaching the point of saying, "I can't." Boys always want to say, "I can do it!" Young men want to prove to themselves, their girlfriend, and the world that "I can!" But God tells you, "You can't." In your own strength, without God, you can't. That is a hard lesson for most of us. You want to be a good Christian—a good pastor. But you will fail over and over until you realize it is only by God's grace that you can follow Jesus. We all fail and need God. Peter knows a young man needs even more grace if he is going to follow Jesus. But to receive that, he has to humble himself.

Are you experiencing God's grace in your life? Do you understand what grace is? Do you show others grace? Or do you demand perfection from them? If you humble yourself before God, you will find grace from both God and others.

We are to humble ourselves under God's mighty hand

Verse 6 says to *Humble yourselves, therefore, under God's mighty hand, that he may lift you up in due time.* We need to make sure we are humbling ourselves under *God's* hand. That may be expressed in submission to others, but submission to God is at the heart of it. As we put our trust in God, we can humble ourselves before others, and the promise is that *God will lift us up.* When? In due time. In *his* time. That usually means waiting longer than you would like, but trust that God knows when the time is right.

As you wait, verse 7 says to *cast all your anxiety on him, because he cares for you*. Often, anxiety causes us to try to lift ourselves up. We are concerned that if we humble ourselves, others will take advantage of us. We won't get that job or make enough money. That girl won't be attracted to a meek, humble man. But exalting yourself is actually unbelief. We don't trust what Jesus said. We don't really believe that God will lift us up. *We* have to do it. So we walk around burdened, anxious, and looking for every chance to exalt ourselves. Humbling yourself means truly trusting God with everything. You can humble yourself without fear of being abused or losing out, because God will take care of you. Cast all your anxiety on God. He is faithful to his word. Grab hold of these beautiful promises! God will lift you up! God will give you grace! God will take care of you!

You may be at a point right now where you have had enough of this humbling business. You have been waiting for God to lift you up and it's not happening. You are beginning to think it is time to lift yourself up. Others are urging you to assert yourself. You are being faced with situations that make it difficult to submit to others. You are feeling more discouraged than ever about making it as a Christian. The trials just keep on coming. Be encouraged. God knows what he is doing! He is probably just exposing another layer of "self" and giving you more opportunities to learn how to humble yourself. Cease striving. Let go. Relax. And know that he is God in a deeper way than ever before.

Chapter 5

Where does God live?

"I live in the high and holy place with those whose spirits are contrite and humble. I restore the crushed spirit of the humble and revive the courage of those with repentant hearts." (Isaiah 57:15)

That is amazing. The God of the universe lives in the most incredible place imaginable. The Bible gives us glimpses of his heavenly home. It is high and holy and glorious. But that is not the only place he lives. He chose to come down and live among us as a man. And even after we crucified him, he still desires to live with us! But not in ornate temples or fancy palaces. He dwells in the hearts of men and women like you and me. We are his temples. During the time he walked this earth, he chose to be born in a humble stable and never had his own home. Isaiah says he lives with the contrite, humble, lowly in spirit, and broken-hearted. The Amplified Bible says it is *the thoroughly penitent, bruised with sorrow for sin.* That sounds like the Beatitudes, where Jesus says the ones who are blessed are the poor in spirit, those who mourn, the meek, and the hungry.

Isaiah warns that if we are not humble, we cannot expect to know God's presence. God uses the experiences that break our hearts to humble us. It is good to be contrite, repentant, humble, lowly in spirit, and broken-hearted, because God longs to dwell in us, and that is the kind of heart he lives in. Something beautiful happens as God takes up residence in our broken hearts. He revives us. Strengthens us. Comforts us. Refreshes us. And gives us new courage.

Chapter 6

False Humility

Is your heart a humble, clean, temple that the Lord of the universe would be pleased to dwell in? Are you experiencing the Lord's healing presence? Unfortunately, I know a lot of Christians who would honestly have to say no. They may be brokenhearted and appear contrite, but only God knows if they are genuinely repentant or truly humble. It is even possible to deceive yourself into thinking you are humble when, in fact, it is false humility. Many Christians fall into the deceptive religious trap set by the enemy. An early church father, Chrysostom, wrote: *There is a strange pride which presents itself as the standard of humility. This false humility is almost wholly the product of self-righteous hypocrisy.*

How can we recognize the false humility that keeps us far from God's presence?

- *Focus on self*. The humble person forgets about himself. By its very nature, humility does not draw attention to itself or talk about itself. The most humble people are often the most conscious of their sin and need for Christ. They don't think they are humble! False humility is a religious façade that may appear humble. The person may talk about how humble they are and genuinely believe they are humble. Paul, in 2 Timothy 3:5, says they have a form of godliness but deny its power. He warns us: Have nothing to do with them, because God has nothing to do with them.

- *Problems with self-esteem.* Instead of a healthy self-concept, they oscillate between feeling that they are nobody who deserves nothing and having an exaggerated sense of self-importance, accompanied by a need for praise and affirmation. The person who exalts himself often has a poor self-image. False humility is not attractive.

- *Not experiencing the grace and freedom of the Spirit.* False humility stops at Romans 7:24: *What a wretched man I am!* He is still under the law, struggling to be a good Christian, and never makes it to Romans 7:25: *Thanks be to God! I am rescued from this body of death through Jesus Christ our Lord!*

- *Difficulty accepting compliments.*

Some examples:

"That was a great sermon!" "Oh, it was nothing. All the glory goes to Christ. It's his word!" Meanwhile, inside, you are grabbing onto every word and hoping for more praise!

"That's a really nice shirt!" "It's old. It was just lying around." Actually, you just bought it and paid a lot for it. You were hoping people would notice it.

"That was an excellent Bible study." "Thanks, but I didn't think it came out too well. I threw it together in a hurry." Actually, you agonized over it for hours, still felt insecure about it, and were hoping for some compliments.

The humble person graciously accepts compliments, but does not rely on them to feed his ego. He enjoys the fruit of his labors while rejoicing with others who do as well. False humility is a manipulative attempt to be praised. It is not honest or genuine. It appears to downplay talents, gifts, and achievements in the hope of gaining even more recognition from others. The truly humble person knows who he is and does not have to prove anything to anyone. He exudes a joy and confidence that is God-given, which others find attractive.

Don't confuse humility with self-hatred, which is destructive. Humility does not mean we beat ourselves up. True humility is realistic. It celebrates our God given abilities while acknowledging our weaknesses. Paul gives us a good example in 1 Corinthians 15:9–10: *For I am the least of the apostles and do not even deserve to be called an apostle because I persecuted the church of God.* If he were to stop there, we could say it was false humility, but he balances it: *But by the grace of God I am what I am, and his grace to me was not without effect. No, I worked harder than all of them – yet not I, but the grace of God that was with me.* Study the life of our Lord Jesus Christ for the best example of a healthy self-image and humility.

If you feel false humility describes you, don't condemn yourself or be discouraged! God is opening your eyes because he loves you and longs to live in you. Part of humbling yourself and growing is being honest about where you are at. God wants to revive your broken heart, refresh you, and give you new courage. It is not easy to find the right balance in being humble, but God will show you if you are slipping into false humility, and he will continue to provide circumstances to truly humble you!

Chapter 7

The Greatest in the Kingdom

One day while I was writing blogs about humility I told the Lord: "I've been on this theme of humility for almost a month now. I have written about it several times. I am sure these folks are tired of hearing about it. I would kind of like something more exciting to share." So the Lord sent me to Matthew 18.

The disciples wanted to know, "Who is the greatest in the kingdom of heaven?" That is pretty exciting, right? How would you answer their question? In your church, who is most important? If you are the pastor, is it you? Who is most important in the Christian community in your city? In this country?

Without knowing what Jesus said, most would probably think of someone on TV. A well-known author. A great evangelist. Someone influential in many churches. A prophet. An apostle. The pastor of a large church.

But Jesus called a child over and had him stand in their midst, and then he said: *"I tell you the truth, unless you change and become like little children, you will never enter the kingdom of heaven. Therefore, whoever humbles himself like this child is the greatest in the kingdom of heaven."*

Wow. That is pretty extreme. We are not only talking about being great in the kingdom. Unless we become like little children, we cannot even *enter* the kingdom. Humbling yourself is not just for the super spiritual. It is a salvation issue.

Jesus provides us with a clear model of how to humble ourselves. It is not just about taking the least important seat at a banquet or giving preference to others. We are to humble ourselves like a child.

I can think of a lot that a child *does not* have:

- He doesn't have much education.
- He isn't married and doesn't have kids.
- He's not independent—he depends on others for everything.
- He doesn't have his own TV program or website.
- He doesn't pastor a church or lead any ministry.
- He doesn't hold a position in government or industry.
- He lacks extensive reasoning ability.

- He doesn't have a complete vocabulary or developed verbal skills.
- He lacks power or physical strength.
- He doesn't think about sex (hopefully...too many children are being exposed to sex at a young age).

So what can we say about a child?

- He loves to play.
- He's not in a hurry.
- He needs teachers to instruct him.
- He doesn't worry about money or where the next meal's coming from.
- He doesn't have a lot of things he *has* to do.
- He needs discipline to guide and protect him. He needs boundaries.
- He takes delight in very simple things.
- He needs a family, a mother and father. Without them, he's vulnerable. He admires, looks up to, and copies his parents and older siblings.
- He's trusting, teachable, and loves learning.
- He likes to know what's expected of him.

So, how can someone change and become a child again? Jesus never asks us to do something impossible. As adults, we can choose to change, to leave everything behind, and become like children.

We can humble ourselves. Jesus is our model. He did it. He left everything to be born as a baby and grow up as a child. More than anyone, he knows it is not easy, but he also knows it is necessary. That is why he said we must be born again. Some sects in New England used to crawl around on the floor in an attempt to obey Jesus' teaching! That's not necessary, but we do need to take Jesus seriously. I am tired of people trying to explain away things Jesus said that make them uncomfortable. I don't think he intends for us to quit our jobs and abandon our family responsibilities, but I do believe he calls us to make some radical changes.

In the verses following that dramatic declaration, Jesus talks more about children:

- We are to receive children in Jesus' name. In doing so, we receive Jesus (18:5).
- Making a child (or someone who has become like a child) sin is very serious (18:6). We should be moved to act on behalf of abused and suffering children.
- We must do anything necessary to overcome sin (to the extreme of cutting off a hand or plucking out an eye) (18:7–9).
- Every child is important to God. We are never to look down on a little one (18:10).
- They have angels in heaven who always have direct access to see the Father's face (18:10).

- Everybody is important to God. It's his will that not a single person would be lost (18:14).
- It's easy for a child to forgive. We need to ensure that we settle our differences with our brothers. Many times, that means humbling ourselves (18:15–17).

It seems to me we are confused. We have got everything backward. Somehow, we have followed the world's standards of importance and success. Like Jesus said (referring to money): *"What is highly valued among men is detestable in God's sight"* (Lk. 16:15).

Chapter 8

How Jesus Humbled Himself

A university in Australia did a study on humility. They found that before Christ, nobody spoke of it as a virtue. Among all the ancient philosophers, Jesus was the first to talk about humbling yourself.

In John 13, Jesus humbled himself and washed the disciples' feet. It is not only an excellent example for us—he commanded us to do the same. There is a key verse that tells us how he was able to do it:

*Jesus knew that the Father had put all things under his power, and that he had come from God, and was returning to God; **so** he got up...* (Jn. 13:3).

Jesus knew three things that enabled him to humble himself:

1.   He knew he had authority. He already knew the Father had put everything in his hands. It was not power or authority he somehow grasped, but the authority given to him by his Father. That knowledge freed him to humble himself and be a servant. He already had everything. There was nothing more to gain by trying to exalt himself. He had nothing to prove. Your Father has also given you authority,

though it is certainly not as much as Jesus had. Knowing that God has given you power and authority here on earth should free you to humble yourself and serve others. You won't lose a thing.

2.   Jesus knew where he came from. He knew his heritage. He knew God sent him with a purpose. He knew he was the Son of God. His identity was secure. Do you know who you are? Do you know anything about your ancestors? Your roots? Do you feel secure in your identity as a Christian? Do you have a deep knowledge of God as your Father? Do you know what it means that you have been adopted as God's son? Do you remember where you came from? The sin and desperation that were part of your life before you met Jesus?

3.   Jesus knew where he was going. He was certain he was returning to God, to his Father, to heaven. He had hope for the future. He knew the cross was not the end. God has a place waiting for you in heaven as well. Do you have a firm hope and confidence in the future God has for you? You are going to share in God's glory!

If you can grab hold of these amazing facts and allow them to impact your life, you will be freed to humble yourself and serve others as Jesus did.

Chapter 9

Ultimate Humility

Jesus demonstrated humility at its extreme: Obedience to the point of dying on the cross.

Philippians 2:1–16 is perhaps the best biblical teaching on humility:

[1]Therefore if you have any encouragement from being united with Christ, if any comfort from his love, if any common sharing in the Spirit, if any tenderness and compassion, [2] then make my joy complete by being likeminded, having the same love, being one in spirit and of one mind. [3] Do nothing out of selfish ambition or vain conceit. Rather, in humility value others above yourselves, [4] not looking to your own interests but each of you to the interests of the others.

In your relationships with one another, have the same mindset as Christ Jesus:

Who, being in very nature God, did not consider equality with God something to be used to his own advantage; [7] rather, he made himself nothing   by taking the very nature of a servant,   being made in human likeness. [8] And being found in appearance as a man,   he humbled himself   by becoming obedient to death—even death on a cross!

⁹ Therefore God exalted him to the highest place   and gave him the name that is above every name, ¹⁰ that at the name of Jesus every knee should bow,   in heaven and on earth and under the earth, ¹¹ and every tongue acknowledge that Jesus Christ is Lord, to the glory of God the Father.

¹² Therefore, my dear friends, as you have always obeyed—not only in my presence, but now much more in my absence—continue to work out your salvation with fear and trembling, ¹³ for it is God who works in you to will and to act in order to fulfill his good purpose.

¹⁴ Do everything without grumbling or arguing, ¹⁵ so that you may become blameless and pure, "children of God without fault in a warped and crooked generation." Then you will shine among them like stars in the sky ¹⁶ as you hold firmly to the word of life. And then I will be able to boast on the day of Christ that I did not run or labor in vain.

Verse 5 commands us to have Christ's attitude, which means following his example and living like he did. The passage shows us various ways his example of humility impacts the way we relate to others:

- Be like-minded, have the same love, and be one in spirit and purpose (v. 2). Living in perfect unity with your brothers and sisters requires a great deal of humility. It means keeping short accounts, truly forgiving others when they offend us, and letting go of resentment. Colossians 3:12–14 pictures it as new "clothes" we put on: Humility, compassion, kindness, gentleness, and patience. We are to forgive as the Lord forgave us, lovingly bearing with each other.

- Do nothing out of vain conceit or selfish ambition (v. 3). Arrogance and ambition can ruin a church, while genuine humility will build it up. Ask God to reveal your heart motives for what you do in church and in the rest of your life.

- Consider (regard, think of) others better than yourself, with an attitude of humility (v. 3). Do you tend to believe you are better than others? Do you look down on people? Do you want to protest: "But I have more experience! I have more education!" That doesn't matter. Humility means we look at others and approach them with the attitude that they are better than we are. Jesus did that! Try it for a while!

- Look out for others' interests. Show genuine concern about what other people are doing and what is important to them. It doesn't mean you cannot look out for your own interests, but put theirs first. We have all had way too much experience putting ourselves first.

How could Jesus do this?

- He did not *consider* his equality with God as something to be grasped (v. 6). He never denied being God. He knew very well who he was. If you have had doubts about Christ's divinity or whether the Bible says he is God, this verse is about as clear as it gets. In very nature, he is God. He is equal to God. All the facts said he was divine, but he ignored them and made the decision to relinquish his position, so he could fully identify with us.

- He made himself nothing, emptied himself, and stripped himself of all the rights and privileges inherent in being God (v. 7). That is extreme, and he did it voluntarily, out of love. He could do it because he trusted his Father to take care of him.

- He took the very nature of a servant. Serving others is at the heart of humility, and Jesus is the supreme example of servanthood. It was not just an act; it was not something he did for a few hours a week as a "service project."

He took the very nature of a servant, and he calls us to do the same.

- He was made in human likeness (v. 8). He humbled himself to the extreme of being born as a baby and sharing in everything it means to be a man, leaving the glory of heaven to live a humble life. He completely identified with us, which he could not do from heaven. If you are serious about humbling yourself, live a humble life. If you really understand the incarnation, you realize it is not about sending a check from your comfortable house to "help the poor." You need to share life with the people you are ministering to. As a prison chaplain, there were times when I wished I could spend a few days living with the inmates to understand what their lives were like. I would enter their world to minister, but then return each night to my home and family. It is like Jesus coming down to teach and perform miracles, and then returning to heaven each night. Jesus became an inmate so he could identify with our bondage, but without sin. (I did get to spend a week living in the cell of a new prison during a training course. The doors were not even locked, but that was enough for me!)

- Humility is expressed in obedience (v. 8). Jesus humbled himself to the extreme of dying the most horrid death possible, the death of the cross.

Verses 9–11 describe how God exalted Jesus to the highest place. Jesus is your guarantee that humbling yourself is worth it, although you are missing the point if the only reason you humble yourself is to be exalted!

Studies of this passage almost always end at verse 11, but verse 12 starts with a "therefore," and as you probably know, you always have to see what that is "there for." Several things should happen as a result of having Christ's attitude of humility:

- Realize how awesome and costly your salvation is. That means taking obedience seriously and working out your salvation with fear and trembling (v. 12). The Amplified Bible says: *Cultivate, carry out to the goal and fully complete - your own salvation with reverence and awe and trembling [self-distrust, that is, with serious caution, tenderness of conscience, watchfulness against temptation; timidly shrinking from whatever might offend God and discredit the name of Christ].*

- Jesus perfectly completed God's will for his life, in the same way we should seek God's will for our lives and carefully carry it out. The NIV says, *"it is God who works in you to will and to act according to his good purpose"* (v. 13). Again, the Amplified clarifies it: *[Not in your own strength] for it is God who is all the while effectually at work in you - energizing and creating in you the power and desire...* God helps us want to do his will, as well as enabling us to do it. Find your place in his plan. If it is humble, accept it. If it is great, give thanks for it humbly and recognize the responsibility that comes with it.

- Do God's will without complaining or arguing. If you follow all he has taught in this chapter, you will shine like stars in our dark world as a blameless, pure child of God, without fault in a crooked and depraved generation (vv. 14–15). You will look like Jesus.

As you can see, there is quite a bit involved in humbling ourselves. It will revolutionize your life. Begin by applying this teaching to your marriage. It could transform it! Re-examine Jesus' life to see how he humbled himself, and follow his example. Let's shine like stars!

Chapter 10

God Will Exalt You

As I finish this book on humbling yourself, Hollywood is presenting the Academy Awards, exalting those they feel were the best performers. Not exactly a display of humility, though some do give lip service to thanking God. It is a long way from what Jesus said several times: *"Everyone who exalts himself will be humbled, and he who humbles himself will be exalted."*

Having examined how to humble yourself, I want to conclude with the reward he promises us, which is far more valuable than any Oscar. If you humble yourself and do your part, then God will do his part. He will lift you up. How? Once again, our example is Jesus, even though no one in this world will ever humble himself as Jesus did. He humbled himself to the extreme, as we saw in Philippians 2. Verse 9 says, *therefore* (Amplified: *because he stooped so low*), as a result of what he did voluntarily:

- God exalted him to the highest place.

- God gave him the name that is above every name.

- Every knee will bow at the name of Jesus, in heaven and on earth and under the earth.

- Every tongue will confess that Jesus Christ is Lord (Phil. 2:9–11).

That is pretty impressive, isn't it? Jesus humbled himself for some thirty-three years to be exalted like this for eternity. Can you ask for anything more? Can you think of anything more the Father could do to exalt his Son?

Your Father has the same heart toward you. He already gave his best, his Son, for your salvation. We don't know the full extent of the reward he has for you, but it does seem to depend on the extent to which you humbled yourself in this life. Jesus said those who exalt themselves have already received their reward in full (Matt. 6:2, 5, 16).

Here is only a small part of what the Bible says is ours:

- No eye has seen, no ear has hear, no mind has conceived what God has prepared for those who love him (1 Cor. 2:9).

- He has made us to be a kingdom and priests to serve his God and Father (Rev. 1:6).

- Jesus and his Father come to us and make their home with us (Jn. 14:23).

- We are going to judge the world (1 Cor. 6:2).

You are assured a reward each time you humble yourself:

- The one who gives a cup of water to a little one certainly will not lose his reward (Matt. 10:42).

- The Father sees when you humble yourself in secret, and will reward you (Matt. 6:18).

- If you are humble (poor, hungry, weeping, or hated by the world), your reward will be great in heaven (Lk. 6:23).

- When you humble yourself, set your pride aside, and love your enemies, doing good to them, you will have a great reward and be called a son of the Most High (Lk. 6:35).

Much of this occurs after death, but there are rewards to be found in this life. You already have all the privileges of a son of the King. 1 Peter 5:6 promises that God will exalt you *in due time*. Trust him with the timing.

If, despite all the Bible teaches, you refuse to humble yourself and instead exalt yourself, God will humble you. Trust me, it is better to humble yourself. Remember that Jesus is the best example of how to do that. If you need another biblical example, Numbers 12:3 states that Moses was the most humble man on earth, yet consider his authority and all that he accomplished. Being humble does not mean you won't do great things for the Lord!

Ultimately, humbling yourself reveals the nature of your faith. Can you wait until you get to heaven to be exalted? Or do you have to get everything now? Can you trust that God will take care of you? To the extreme that Jesus went, trusting that he would be okay as a baby in a filthy stable? Do you know who you are in Christ? Or are you still relying on things in this world to make you feel like someone with value? Don't get overly focused on humbling yourself. Focus on Jesus. As you love him and walk with him, you will find your heart changed, and without even realizing it, you will surprise yourself with your submission, obedience, and service. Don't be afraid of becoming like a child.

www.ingramcontent.com/pod-product-compliance
Lightning Source LLC
Chambersburg PA
CBHW060610030426
42337CB00018B/3029